Animal Builders

Wild World

Animal Builders

by Dr. Jim Flegg with
Eric & David Hosking

Newington Press

FRONT COVER: A HARVEST MOUSE LOOKS OUT FROM THE SAFETY OF ITS NEST.
BACK COVER: A LONG-TAILED TIT WORKS HARD TO BUILD ITS NEST.
TITLE PAGE: THE OPENINGS OF TUBES BUILT BY MARINE WORMS.

First published in the United States in 1991 by Newington Press
2 Old New Milford Road
Brookfield, Connecticut 06804

Text copyright © Dr. Jim Flegg 1990
Photographs copyright © David and Eric Hosking and the Frank Lane Picture Agency 1990 and individual copyright holders on the following pages: T. and P. Gardner 16, Roger Hosking 7 (bottom), 10, G. E. Hyde 25 (both), Mark Newman 20, 21, L. Perkins 22, Fritz Polking 9 (left), Silvestris 23, 24, Phil Ward 11, D. P. Wilson (title page), Martin Withers (cover)

First published in Great Britain in 1990 by Belitha Press Limited

Library of Congress Cataloging-in-Publication Data
Flegg, Jim
Animal builders/Jim Flegg with Eric & David Hosking Brookfield, Conn.: Newington Press, 1991.
32 p.: col. ill.; cm (Wild world)
Includes bibliographical references (p. 29)
How animals, fish, and insects build their homes and keep them safe from predators and the forces of nature.
1. Animals—Habitations—Juvenile literature.
I. Hosking, Eric John.   II. Hosking, David.
III. Title   IV. Series
ISBN: 1-878137-05-0   591.564

Words in **bold** are defined in the glossary.

A building site.

Contents

Animal Builders	7
Nest Builders	8
Sculptors in Paper and Clay	12
Above and Below Ground	14
Plasterers	18
Engineers	20
Underwater Builders	22
Stronger than Steel	24
The Great Tunnel Builders	26
Glossary	28
For Further Reading	29
Index	30

Animal Builders

Watching builders (the human sort) at work, we marvel not only at their skills—the way that the bricks are laid to a precise pattern, the fact that walls are vertical, floors horizontal, and roofing tiles overlap so neatly to keep out the rain—but also at the technology that backs them up. Depending on the size of the job, there will be excavators, hammer drills, laser beam levelers, tungsten steel chisels, and measurements taken with tapes accurate to a fraction of an inch. These are all used by people with years of training and experience to produce the final expert job. Nor should we forget the engineers and architects, who designed the job in the first place. They make sure that it will be suitable for its intended purpose and that it will fit well into its environment.

But *should* we be so proud of our own skills? How does nature set about *its* building tasks? In *Wild World,* you will discover that, almost always, nature got there first! The precision structure of a wasps' nest was achieved without measuring instruments; the beaver's dam was built without mechanical diggers. Tiny marine worms build strong chalky tubes that form massive reeflike structures that can withstand the force of tropical seas. You will see air conditioning installed in termite nests; precision temperature and **humidity** control by mallee fowl; spiders using fibers stronger than steel—and much more that really does make us think and marvel.

The combs in a wasps' nest.

A spider's web covered in dew.

A male Ruppell's weaver at its nest. *A male satin bowerbird in its bower.*

Nest Builders

The powers of flight that make birds so successful were not gained during their evolution without some cost. When their "arms" became wings, birds lost the hands that many animals, including ourselves, find so useful. Imagine the problems of building a nest with just a beak and feet! The hanging basket nest of Ruppell's weaver—made of strips of palm leaf, torn off, knotted, and neatly woven—is one of the marvels of the natural world. The weavers are the masters among an impressive group of bird builders. Hanging free, the nests enjoy any cooling breeze to soften the burning African sun. They are designed so that eggs or young cannot fall out or be reached by **predatory** snakes and lizards.

The showy male satin bowerbird builds one of the most complicated and beautiful of all bird constructions. It consists of a passageway of twigs, set upright on the ground, and may be 3 feet (1 meter) long. This "bower" is decorated by the male with leaves, berries, and flowers—usually blue in color—all designed to attract a mate. Often a twig with bluish sap will be used to daub "paint" on the walls. Near Australian **outback** homes, the bowerbirds happily use colored scraps of paper, cans, plastic cups, and broken china or glass as decoration. But the bower is built *only* to attract the female. Once mating has occurred, she goes off to build a proper nest, lay eggs, and raise her young.

A pair of great crested grebes at their nest.

A long-tailed tit outside its nest.

No matter how hard it rains or how quickly the floodwater rises, the floating nest of the great crested grebe always stays safe. Built as a raft of reeds and other water plants, the nest is anchored securely to nearby plants out in the lake. So although it can rise and fall with changes in the water level, it does not drift away. Grebes are supremely well adapted to water life. For powerful swimming, their legs are set back near their stubby tails. This makes them very clumsy when walking, so the gently sloping edges of the nest allow them to slip on and off without difficulty. Before she leaves, the female grebe covers the eggs with waterweeds to hide them from marauding crows.

Protected from **predators** deep in a thorny thicket, the long-tailed tit's pouch-shaped nest is a masterpiece of construction work. The main structure is of horsehair and spiders' webs, with moss and feathers for **insulation**. There may be as many as 2,000 feathers in the nest, each one brought on a separate flight! Outside, the nest is camouflaged with patches of **lichen** taken from tree trunks. As the brood of nestlings grows—and there may be as many as ten—they can wriggle around without difficulty, as the nest walls are flexible as well as strong. The breeding pair may be helped in raising their young by relatives—perhaps their brothers and sisters, or youngsters from an earlier nest.

A hibernating common dormouse.

Few mammals **hibernate**, but the dormouse is one that does. During the autumn, it feeds all hours of the day and night, especially on berries rich in sugar. The little dormouse gets fatter and fatter. While still active, it builds a nest of grasses and leaves, shaped like an untidy ball of string, deep in brambles or a hollow tree. When it is so fat that it can hardly move, the dormouse snuggles into its nest. **Insulated** against the cold, it settles down for the winter. Hibernation is more than just sleeping. To save precious energy, the dormouse's temperature, heartbeat, and breathing rates drop to such an extent that it seems lifeless. In this way, it can survive on its body fat for up to four months, until the warmth of spring brings it back to life.

Very few of the larger mammals show any inclination to build, let alone any skills as construction workers. The great apes, our closest animal relations, possess hands very similar to our own. They have thumbs and fingers that can be used to grasp with great delicacy, but even *they* do little in the way of building. The exception is the gorilla, roaming in family groups through the mountain forests of tropical Africa. Every night, each gorilla builds itself a nest. Often high in the trees, these platforms are crudely made from broken-off leafy branches and offer some shelter from the cold mountain air. They also offer some protection to a young gorilla from any **predator** brave enough to tackle it with the huge silverback male gorilla resting nearby.

A male mountain gorilla grooming a female.

The strong cells of a wasps' nest protect the grubs.

Sculptors in Paper and Clay

In spring, the queen wasp sets out to found a new **colony**. Choosing a sheltered cavity, often in the roof of a house, she builds her nest. This nest is made of chewed wood fiber, the wasp version of papier mâché. It is paper thin but quite rigid. Little bigger than a table tennis ball to start with, it is often as big as a football by the end of the summer. Beneath the spherical outer case are clustered rows of cells, each with six sides. Hexagonal tubes such as these are very strong. We use similar tubes to reinforce lightweight doors and to give extra strength to the double skin of aircraft. Worker wasps are raised in these cells. They in turn take over nest building, rasping dry bark and other fibers from nearby trees or woodwork with their jaws and mixing them with saliva. Meanwhile the queen gets on with her prime task of egg laying.

With its banana-shaped beak and grotesquely long legs and neck, it is surprising that the flamingo can build a nest at all, let alone the elegant structure that it does create out of mud. Shaped like the cone of a volcano, flamingo nests hold the eggs high enough above the mud to keep them safe from sudden floods following a storm. Having a tall nest also helps the female flamingo when it comes to **incubation**, as it gives her room enough to fold her immensely long legs and settle her body comfortably into the cup. Once the young have hatched, they gather in large groups to roam over the mudflats while their parents hunt for tiny shrimps and water plants. These they sieve from the water with their extraordinary banana-shaped beaks. Each parent, returning with food, somehow manages to recognize its own chick in this milling, squabbling, hungry mob.

Adult and young greater flamingoes stand by their nests.

Termite mounds can be very large.

Above and Below Ground

Termite mounds are far from simple heaps of earth. They are expertly built, air-conditioned castles that are set hard by the tropical sun. Each **colony** of these antlike insects consists of a queen, millions of workers, and many "soldiers" with huge jaws, whose job is to defend the castle and its occupants. The mound's above-ground section often towers higher than a person, while underground tunnels penetrate deep into the earth. It is hollow, funneling hot air out like a chimney to cool the inside.

One Australian termite builds mounds flattened from side to side, with the thinnest edge facing the midday sun to keep heating to a minimum. The longer sides face north and south so accurately that these are called compass termites. The workers emerge after dark to feed on grass. Australians say that the termites eat more grass each day than all the cattle, sheep, and kangaroos grazing on it put together!

Human builders sometimes use simple mud. These multistory apartments were built from mud over 600 years ago in Mareb, Yemen. They were set hard by the baking hot sun and have withstood the weather ever since. They are still lived in even today. Rain is unusual in the Arabian peninsula, but when it rains, it rains hard. Sand, whipped up by stormy desert winds, can be just as **abrasive** as a grindstone. The buildings really are tough. In many tropical countries, bricks are still made in the sun, often with bits of straw for extra strength. Elsewhere, the process has been modernized, and huge coal, gas, or oil-fired ovens are used to fire and bake even stronger bricks.

Six-story mud buildings in Yemen.

During the autumn and winter, pairs of chickenlike mallee fowl of Australia collect massive heaps of leaves. The male and female work together to scrape the leaves into a hole they have dug, which may be 3 feet (1 meter) deep and several yards across. The leaf pile is moistened by rain and may weigh 100 tons or more. As it begins to rot, it generates heat. In this mound, the hen digs a nest chamber and lays about twenty eggs, which she covers with leaves. These are **incubated** by the heat of the rotting mound, so it is vital that, for the next two months, the mallee fowl test the temperature regularly with their beaks. They can do this very accurately, adding a covering of soil to keep off too much sun or scraping the soil away if the nest is too cool.

Mallee fowl build huge nest mounds.

Cave swiftlets build their nests high on cave walls.

Deep underground in gigantic caves in the remotest parts of Southeast Asia, hundreds of thousands of cave swiftlets share a gloomy home with bats. Unlike the bats, the swiftlets hunt in daylight. They are nearly always on the wing, for swiftlets have such long wings that they land only on their nests. While hunting insects, the cave swiftlets may also catch feathers and seeds drifting on the wind. Back at their cave, they mix the seeds and feathers with large quantities of sticky saliva, which sets like glue. With this mixture they construct neat, cup-shaped nests, stuck to tiny ledges on the cave walls. These are strong enough to hold eggs and, later, nestlings. The nests have an even more unusual use. Many are collected by local people for what is now a big business, the manufacture of birds-nest soup.

A male yellow-billed hornbill feeds a female hidden in the nest.

Plasterers

In Africa and Asia where hornbills live, there are many **predators**—like lizards, snakes, and monkeys—that can climb trees. Hornbills are big birds and nest in large natural holes in trees. The nests are so large that any predator could easily reach in. To protect the **incubating** female once she is sitting on her eggs, the male plasters up the entrance with mud. He leaves just one hole so small that only the tip of her beak can poke out to take the food he brings her. Once the eggs have hatched and the young are a couple of weeks old, the female breaks through the mud wall. The pair then replace it, again leaving only a tiny hole through which they feed their young. As each youngster is ready to leave the nest, the wall is demolished and rebuilt—those still inside helping those outside with the task.

Carpenters

Behind its neat circular entrance hole, the great spotted woodpecker excavates a deep, bottle-shaped nest in a tree trunk—usually in living timber. It does this by pecking away at the wood with its strong beak. "Why don't woodpeckers get terrible headaches?" is the obvious question to ask. The woodpecker avoids this problem by having a pad of spongy **tissue** as a shock absorber between beak and skull. Also, it doesn't attack the wood like a road drill, relying only on force. It uses its beak like a chisel, twisting off flakes of wood a little at a time. Safe from **predators** deep in the nest, young woodpeckers are among the ugliest of all small birds. They look almost like small prehistoric pterodactyls.

A male great spotted woodpecker by the entrance to its nest.

Beavers work hard to build their dams.

A beaver at work.

Engineers

Perhaps more than any other animal, the beaver is able to change the landscape in which it lives. By building their dams across forest streams, beavers create pools and even lakes and swamps where once there was dry land. The dam, made of branches and large, heavy logs, is a massive barrier—and an amazing feat

of engineering. It contains the beavers' "lodge," with living chambers that are reached by underwater entrances in the newly formed lake. Because beavers are expert swimmers, this creates no difficulties and gives them safety from **predators**. Beavers are vegetarians and have powerful jaw muscles and huge front teeth. The teeth grow continually as they wear down. They have hard brown **enamel** at the front and softer enamel behind. As they wear away, the tips become shaped like chisels—very effective tools for felling trees and cutting branches.

A male three-spined stickleback by its nest.

Underwater Builders

The male stickleback builds his nest of fine strands of weed and **algae** close to the base of a tuft of waterweed. It is out of the main force of the stream but with plenty of oxygen-rich water flowing through. In spring, his belly changes color to bright red, and he keeps watch on his nest, performing a complex, weaving "dance" to attract a mate. Once a female has come close, he lures her right into his newly built nest. There she lays her eggs, which he **fertilizes**. She then goes away to feed and get back into top condition after having produced all those eggs. He is left to stand guard over his one-parent family, until the eggs hatch and the small fish disperse to feed in the shelter of the waterweed.

Only one member of the enormous spider family (there are about 40,000 different species worldwide) spends most of its life underwater, the aptly named water spider. The water spider, which can be ¾ inch (2 centimeters) long, chooses relatively still freshwater ponds with plenty of waterweed. It first spins an underwater bell-shaped web, attached to nearby **aquatic** plants and so finely woven as to be airtight. The spider then makes a series of visits to the surface, each time trapping a layer of air between the hairs on its body. It brings this air back to release into the web as an oxygen store in its own private "diving bell." It lives and lays its eggs inside the bell, emerging only on hunting expeditions or to replace its air supplies.

A water spider with its diving bell.

An orb web spider tends its trap.

Stronger than Steel

Spiders produce the silk for their webs from glands near the base of their **abdomen**. The silk emerges as a liquid, to be spun into threads by spinnerets, small organs near the **anus**. Orb web spiders use a roughly circular web to catch flying insects, setting it across a likely gap between plants. Each species has a different web design, and each uses threads of various strengths in its construction. The strongest threads are, size for size, stronger than the best steel wire. Some threads are sticky, to trap insects. The spider waits on a leaf nearby, one leg touching the web to sense the slightest vibration when prey is caught. Then it rushes out to subdue its victim with a bite from its poison fangs, wrapping it in more silk to eat later.

So useful is the fine, strong silk spun by the silk moth caterpillar that today silk moths are more common in captivity than in the wild. Over much of Asia, they are raised in millions, feeding furiously and growing rapidly on a diet of mulberry leaves. After several molts to change its always over-stretched skin, the caterpillar becomes sluggish and ready to **pupate**. For protection, it spins a silken cocoon. Safe inside, the **pupa** undergoes amazing body changes. The fat caterpillar that entered emerges as a beautiful moth. The cocoon contains thousands of yards of silken thread, and on commercial farms this cocoon offers no protection from man. Batches of cocoons are boiled to kill the pupae and loosen the threads, which are then spun onto bobbins, dyed, and used in the production of fine fabrics.

Common silk moth cocoons—one has been opened to show the pupa inside.   Above is the adult moth.

The Great Tunnel Builders

Broad, muscular shoulders and short, strong limbs make the badger an ideal tunnel digger. Badger feet are wide and are equipped with strong claws for scooping out the earth with all the efficiency of a mechanical excavator. Badgers live in groups in a complex underground network of tunnels and chambers, often called a *set*. Some sets have been in existence for over a century. The tons of earth that the badgers have dug out make massive earthwork mounds, crisscrossed by well-trodden badger pathways. Some chambers are used as bedrooms—badgers often sleep for days on end in cold weather. The dry leaves, grass, and ferns they use for bedding are dragged to the tunnel mouth for airing on warm days.

A badger by the entrance to its set.

A rabbit looks out from its burrow.

☐ Rabbits, too, dig out large networks of tunnels to form their *warrens.* An old, established warren will contain several hundred yards of interconnecting tunnels and breeding chambers. The tunnel floor is of earth packed hard by the treading of countless rabbit feet. This is a useful communications network if a fox or other predator attacks. Sentry rabbits thump their large back feet on the ground to sound the alarm, and the tunnels carry the warning all over the warren.

A human-built tunnel.

☐ Many other animals dig tunnels—in earth as soft as sand or even as hard as clay. Tunnels offer shelter from bad weather and provide a safe place to give birth and raise young. Although **primitive** peoples used caves for these purposes, tunneling (usually for roads or railways) is a feature of modern engineering. In soil, tunnels dug by humans need a lining of steel or concrete to prevent collapse. People with machines can drill or blast tunnels through solid rock—a feat that large animals cannot equal. However, amazingly enough, some smaller animals, especially small burrowing shellfish, use their powerfully **acid** saliva to drill tunnels in solid limestone rocks, equaling their human counterparts!

Glossary

abdomen the belly
abrasive able to rub or wear away a surface
algae (singular = alga) certain simple plants that live mostly in water
anus the opening of the body through which solid waste is passed
aquatic living or growing in or near water
acid a chemical substance with a sour taste that often reacts strongly with other substances
colony a number of animals of the same kind living together
enamel the hard, smooth coating of the teeth
fertilize to make fertile—to make fruitful and productive
hibernation a sleeplike, inactive state in which body functions such as breathing and heart rate slow down. Some animals spend the winter in hibernation.
humidity moisture or dampness
incubation keeping eggs warm in order to hatch them
insulation something that protects from heat or cold
lichens certain simple plants growing on rocks, trees, etc.
outback areas of Australia where few people live
predator an animal that lives by hunting other animals for food
primitive the earliest or simplest form of something
pupa (plural = pupae) the stage of an insect's life when it changes into an adult. At this stage it is usually completely still and does not feed
pupate to become a *pupa*
sculptor someone who makes or models something using different materials
tissue what an animal or plant is made up of

For Further Reading

Amazing Animal Builders
    by Annette Tison and Talus Taylor
    (Putnam, 1989)

Animal Architects
    Edited by Donald J. Crump
    (National Geographic Society, 1987)

The Beaver
    by Hope Ryden
    (Putnam, 1986)

Home: How Animals Find Comfort & Safety
    by Laurence Pringle
    (Scribner, 1987)

Spiders
    by Jane Dallinger
    (Lerner Publications, 1988)

Vanishing Habitats
    By Noel Simon
    (Gloucester, 1987)

Index

A
Algae (singular—alga), 22, 28

B
Badger set, 26
Beaver dam, 7, 20, 21
Bowerbird, 8
Brick structures, 15
Building materials
   algae, 22
   branches, 11, 20
   clay, 12
   earth, 14, 26
   feathers, 9, 17
   horsehair, 9
   leaves, 8, 10, 16
   moss, 9
   mud, 13, 15, 18
   paper, 12
   seeds, 17
   silk, 24, 25, 26
   spiders' webs, 9
   twigs, 8

C
Cave swiftlet nests, 17
Colony, 28
   of termites, 14
   of wasps, 12

D
Dormouse, 10

F
Fertilization, 28
   of stickleback eggs, 22
Flamingo nests, 13

G
Gorilla nest, 11
Great crested grebe, 9

H
Hibernation, 28
   of dormouse, 10
Hornbill *see* Yellow-billed hornbill

I
Incubation, 13, 28
   of flamingo eggs, 13
   of mallee fowl eggs, 16
   of yellow-billed hornbill eggs, 18
Insulation
   of dormouse nest, 10
   of long-tailed tit nest, 9

L
Lichen, 28
Long-tailed tit, 9

M
Mallee fowl nests, 16
Mud structures, 15

N
Nest
    of cave swiftlet, 17
    of dormouse, 10
    of flamingo, 13
    of gorilla, 11
    of grebe, 9
    of long-tailed tit, 9
    of mallee fowl, 16
    of stickleback, 22
    of wasps, 12
    of weaver birds, 8
    of woodpecker, 19
    of yellow-billed hornbill, 18

O
Orb web spider, 24

P
Predators, 8, 9, 11, 18, 19, 21, 28

R
Rabbit warren, 27

S
Set, badger, 26
Silk
    of silk moth caterpillar, 25
    of spider web, 24
Silk moths
    pupae of, 25
    raising, 25

Spider webs, 7
    material of, 24
    of orb web spider, 24
    of water spider, 23
Stickleback nest, 22
Structural precision
    of beaver dam, 7
    of wasps' nest, 7

T
Temperature control
    in dormouse nest, 10
    in long-tailed tit nests, 9
    in mallee fowl nests, 16
    in termite mounds, 14
    in weaver bird nests, 8
Termite mounds, 14
Tit *see* Long-tailed tit
Tunnels
    of badgers, 26
    of humans, 27
    of rabbits, 27

W
Warren, rabbit, 27
Water spider, 23
Wasps' nest, 7, 12
Weaver birds, 8
Woodpecker nest, 19

Y
Yellow-billed hornbill nests, 18